PRAISE FOR
To Pay for Our Next Breath

"Alfonso Zapata's debut performance, *To Pay for Our Next Breath*, enters the world singing in every key while simultaneously dancing across and down the page. Both Prince and Michael Jackson would be proud. This meticulously curated mixtape of poems moves with visual and aural precision accompanied by Selena, D'Angelo, Club Nouveau and the Foo Fighters, while Bill Withers, Linda Ronstadt, Aaron Neville and K-Ci & JoJo sing back up. The satisfying sequential poems like, 'The Writer Attempts to Paint' and 'Leaving My Abuelos' Basement' are as brilliantly executed as the formal dexterity Zapata exhibits through three expertly crafted sections of prose, erasure, ghazals and more. Every exit and final line in this collection lands with such precision, Zapata can no longer hide behind the 'who invited him' to the party. This poet is our new Prom King!"

—FRANK X WALKER, author of *Load In Nine Times*

"In Alfonso Zapata's superb debut collection, *To Pay for Our Next Breath*, we are taken masterfully into the complicated world of family, through honest and detailed exploration of memory and Zapata's keen attention to detail. He seamlessly integrates the Spanish language into the lines of his poems, each carefully crafted and finely-honed. Zapata's narratives are wide-ranging in poetic form and in subject, giving us a wonderfully unique and intimate look into the life of one Mexican American Midwest family (his own). The voice here is unfailingly likable, often tremendously funny, and always, *always*, heartbreakingly honest."

—JULIA JOHNSON, author of *Subsidence*

T0349364

"The band's all here. Some dressed in dance sweat, others performing in the mists of the rafters. In this must-read collection, *To Pay for Our Next Breath*, Zapata details to how to build a life in the shadows of totems. He invites us to join the chorus of family and love."

—DAMARIS B. HILL, author of *A Bound Woman Is a Dangerous Thing*

To Pay for Our Next Breath

To Pay for Our Next Breath

Poems

Alfonso Zapata

The TRP Southern Poetry Breakthrough Series
Kentucky

 ★trp

TRP: THE UNIVERSITY PRESS OF SHSU
HUNTSVILLE, TEXAS 77341

Library of Congress Cataloging-in-Publication Data

Names: Zapata, Alfonso, 1996- author.
Title: To pay for our next breath : poems / Alfonso Zapata.
Other titles: TRP Southern poetry breakthrough series.
Description: First edition. | Huntsville, Texas : TRP: The University Press
    of SHSU, [2025] | Series: The TRP Southern poetry breakthrough series:
    Kentucky
Identifiers: LCCN 2024028123 (print) | LCCN 2024028124 (ebook) | ISBN
    9781680034141 (trade paperback) | ISBN 9781680034158 (ebook)
Subjects: LCSH: Arts and society--Poetry. | Crisis management--Poetry. |
    Humanity in art--Poetry. | Creation (Literary, artistic, etc.)--Poetry.
    | Immortality (Philosophy)--Poetry. | LCGFT: Poetry.
Classification: LCC PS3626.A6386 T6 2025 (print) | LCC PS3626.A6386
    (ebook) | DDC 813/.6--dc23/eng/20240624
LC record available at https://lccn.loc.gov/2024028123
LC ebook record available at https://lccn.loc.gov/2024028124

FIRST EDITION

Front cover image by Shutterstock | octopusaga
Author photo by Alfonso Zapata

Cover design by Cody Gates, Happenstance Type-O-Rama
Interior design by Maureen Forys, Happenstance Type-O-Rama

Printed and bound in the United States of America
First Edition Copyright: 2025

TRP: The University Press of SHSU
Huntsville, Texas 77341
texasreviewpress.org

The TRP Southern Poetry Breakthrough Series
Series Editor: J. Bruce Fuller

The TRP Southern Poetry Breakthrough Series highlights a debut full-length collection by emerging authors from each state in the southern United States.

In memory of Alfonso Zapata Sr., Papi Poncho
1942–2023

CONTENTS

I

II

III

I

Como me Duele

After *Selena: Live From The Astrodome (1995)*

wringing runs from *perder*, she lives
in my padrinos' playlist, synths shining

> she's twenty-three here so that's
> the version that we get to remember

her voice slick as gliss, bookending
bassline slides, chords chopped close

> guitarists, singers, drummers in all black
> to let her explode in front of them

here with tio's silver piped shirts
gut scrubbing polish off belt buckle tops

> her immortal cross chest glowing unfaded
> magenta, this dress a Halloween costume

she sings, we laugh at card games, bad plays
grandparents yell about my sloppy shuffles

> her family band knows they're out
> of focus for the broadcast, for her stage

hands unable to form the bridge
on their own, over Selena's last song

sixty-seven thousand pairs of ears circling
the performers, all tuned to her finale

but she is far from this moment. we know
she's dead in a month but here it's different

she doesn't know yet, so as cymbals
shatter she shouts *hasta luego*, see you later

the little details are what we have to latch onto;
a bandaged index, her husband's showoff solo

and now there's a grimness behind the firework
pop and flash, smoke wafting as she waves to us

we will always interrupt ourselves
to reanimate her; when she says *ayudame*

help me, I know loss, I know pain
you do too, say it with me, con animo

she means us, we'll drop conversation
to come to her, to be her voice, together now:

ay ay ay, como me duele

Dendrochronology and the Art of Notetaking

I have taken the ballpoint pen
for granted. When it was all
quills and inkwells, every flourish
was an effort, an extra viscous dip
and risk of blotting your blotter.
I have the privilege of not thinking

about the curls of my I's, a drawstring
snap turning a T into one stroke,
these free fixations distinct like fingerprints.
We varicose notebooks, carve them
like tree rings and commit to a memory,
the way dog-eared novels diagnose

the past. *This ring tells of a wildfire*
decades ago; this fold tells of a reader
so startled by a revelation that the book
had to be put down for the night.
These pages, corners folded and greased
with palm sweat and cat spit,

will end up a bargain in an estate sale,
our little habits, unthoughts
outlasting us the way
a grandparent
will someday only be
remembered by the scent
of their perfume

Leaving My Abuelos' Basement, Christmas Eve 2022

Accompanied by Cielito Lindo Huasteco

It's cold down here
but this is where we kids go

every cousin squeezed in
to cracked plastic children's chairs

we talk with wide gestures
swing inked arms wild

to liven the place up.
Bass once bled

through the drop ceiling
my tia's buzzed cackle

rattling through the vent.
The playlists are softer now

Papi Poncho heads to bed at nine
we pull him up, he trails

his oxygen tank to the door for the night.
When dinner's done we step upstairs into the clouds

of masa harina and the sweat stuck kitchen
shake thin salt from little roosters

singe fingertips peeling tortillas
from greased comals

nestle rice onto hot pot holders
ignore the living room's new bedpan.

Cielito Lindo appears
as it always does

we sync *ay ay ay ay*'s

but now there's one fewer
in the chorus

and I imagine a quiet
swelling up

once midnight hits
we drive fifteen minutes home.

I drive five hours home
and now I know how it feels

from the inside to watch
a band breaking up.

Moving A Hospital Bed Into
The Living Room

It's supposed to be improvement,
break from the hospital's unfamiliar,
but it's only extension, long arm
reaching from examination room
to grandparents' house, reminder.
Still, we know he'll be happier home,
no matter how unwell it'll become.
So we let bulging wires trace walls
and weave between family photos
like deflating veins, infect the hallways,
turned sick and long. We adapt to the stick
of bedside-table rubber. Allow the oxygen
tank permanent residence in the corner.
My grandmother will sleep on the couch
next to him, but won't let it become her bed.
Will always move pillows and blankets
from closet to sofa,
from sofa to closet,
believing that this
will be temporary.
I hoped she was right.

A Dedication

Admire the apple corer, the specific
tool: post-driver, wick cutter, rice
cooker and its slow rumble, the -ers
of single advertised use, how titles
seem to signify it all, how bits
of materials configured in such
a way can narrow their purpose
from infinite to one. Or so
the packaging says: the corer can
peel, a wick cutter can clip roaches,
titles just an assignment.

My grandfather, trying to bounce back
from pneumonia, tubed and tanked,
asks about the air pressure of my tires.

After telling me how thin I've become
since cutting back on the Blue Moon,
my grandmother hands me her bottle
of Corralejo, brown liquor in sapphire
and amber, to have me pour us shots.

The first time I understood
my father was a weekend,
watching him squint through
a wet windshield's bokeh,
strap cargo against wind,
sink tent-poles into muck,
bail floodwater from his kayak,
was seeing him see it through.

My mother details the satisfaction
of a well-timed vacuum: the crackle
of dust and cat litter crammed into
plastic chambers, compressed into loaves,
fill, expunge, again, again, silence
the sign that it's finished, the way
an open book abandoned will close itself.

The -ers carry invisible weight,
cumbersome as design docs, hefting
them over bruising shoulders
to lighten loads. When we leave, the -ers
can become raw material again,
become an expanded infinite
carrying less and less every hour.
I ask of them one more thing: teach me
how to carry the weight someday too.
Stay hydrated, yes mother.
Lift with your legs, yes father.

Untitled

My name stretches three
before me. The one Zapata, a father,
roots transplanted carefully

by the second, hands brick
hard and red, from one country's
soil to another's, deep and black.

The third, a campesino hero,
bandoliered and dead young,
no blood between him and me

but the same starting point.
My family has never called me
Alfonso. It's reserved for the elders.

To them I'm AJ, grandfathered
initials, shortchanged a syllable
at Christmas parties.

And I, in classrooms, heard that name
called for attendance, after a long line
of names that blur,

last in the roll,
and it feels like
it couldn't possibly
be for me.

Leaving My Abuelos' Basement, Christmas Eve 2015

Accompanied by **Cielito Lindo Huasteco**

It's cold down here
but this is where we kids go

running out of seats on ever polished tile
leaning cool against wobbling wood walls

us cousins talk and I drone tired, sitting slouched
on an exercise ball after my Meijer shift

of scrubbing mold from produce misters
but energy buzzes from our cluster.

Up there someone kicks a bottle
and stomps shake the drop ceiling

the circular tromps of someone trying
to dance with the jaunt of norteño.

Mami la screams down *vente arriba*
y juga treinta y uno and slams the door

so I sling myself up those stairs
with all the other tired men because

who am I to refuse the slap
of hunched playing cards

on the still tacky lacquer of the table.
Papi Poncho is wired, thick mustache

freshly dyed in that too noticeable way
retired and refusing to stop wearing coveralls

and he offers the room, even me,
heavy glasses amber-tinted with tequila.

And as we sync at *ay ay ay ay*
canta y no llores

I take my first shot
with people who love me.

I'm offered licks of lime and salt
to soften the sizzle of sinuses

and the back jaw tingle but
I refuse because I want to be able

to get used to this, to be their type of strong,
to make this a tradition, to ascend

like all the other Alfonsos in the room,
to believe that we all will last

Peeling

Mom insists that I wear a sleeveless.
I resist, don't own one, don't want
anybody to see the white sheen
of biceps which haven't seen
daylight in who knows how long.
She insists, hands me one of my dad's,
a used-to-be beige, sweat bleached.
I don't want to do this. Still,
dad and I climb the ladder, ignore
the "do not proceed past this" rung
and stretch onto the roof. Our loadout:

> a dumpster offside the garage,
> green and yawning;

> tens of buckets from every hardware store
> in the state, full of prybars and hammers;

> yellow leather gloves, sap stained
> from the bleed of felled trees;

> two iron ice scrapers, peeling
> shingles for the pale roof.

Neither of us sunscreened;
that was the Mexican in us,
his full and my half, burn-proofed
by genetics. But father and son,
side by side in sunlight

look like a tv set's contrast test,
perfect dark and perfect light.
We kneel down onto the boil of shingles,
shining like fish scales, and work.
Hours pass, water bottles tossed up
between hammer drives, backwash
evaporating in plastic chambers.
I reflect, rejected sun blooming
off arms, legs, stiff hands.
I tire early, lie against the pitch
of a vaulted ceiling, skin shadowed
by a chimney, while he chips away
absorbs light, holds it in every scar.
Eventually we finish, descend, I look down
and my arms are just a bit darker.

On Felling Sixteen Dying Trees

Another white pine leans after a wind–
storm whistles through split trunks

pinecones falling into floodwater
floating up and skirting dirty puddles

and dad's layed off this week so
he decides the whole treeline must go.

He points out trunks, flayed
nude, pockmarked and hollow, *now*

those holes aren't just on the outside,
they're all through them, these trees

are sponges and I don't want to get
sued when one tips over and hits a shed.

When we tore down the trees
every limb was sap stuck

forearm tats tacky with the stuff
pockets glued shut as each cut

coughed a last gasping phlegm.
He rents a woodchipper for the day, hands me

guide wires tied high as the ladder could reach
and I remember muscle, the dominant

chainsaw cutting wedges and my pull
toppling trees as old as him, as old

as his father when he was born.
We lift and slide them

into a mulching mouth.
In the still sore next week we ground

all the little stumps, erased traces
tracked roots like arteries

severed them with mattock swings
planted saplings.

We laid soaker hoses
staked fertilizer

both of us hoping
the new could survive the storms

longer than the old.

Leaving My Abuelos' Basement, Christmas Eve 1999

Accompanied by Cielito Lindo Huasteco

The cold of the first one I remember
is a frozen moment, posed photos

of children waiting to be taken
in pastel chairs smiling lost-tooth grins

we're shining hands passing Nintendo controllers
we jump with Mario hoping we'll fly with him

here the ceiling is cosmically tall
we leap to reach its moon crags

and graze heaven with fingernails
in the basement where I was

conceived, where I was *not*
an accident but a surprise

to young parents deep in bottles.
I feel like I've never left here

like I never want to, but I'm hand held
hoisted over a shoulder up steep stairs.

Every Alfonso is Poncho but I
am not Alfonso, I'm AJ or *ay-yay*, as they say

Alfonso is reserved for men with creased eyes
with soul-patches with darkened hands.

They sing in a language I will not be taught
drink from fizzed bottles I can't touch

I sit on the laps of these gods and am told
one day mijo, one day, like divinity can be earned

and I cry imagining poncho, wondering
what happens to one when another ascends.

They sing and I don't know the words yet
but I know *ay ay ay ay* and the rest

seem to mean everything to them.
Canta y no llores

por que cantando se alegran,
cielito lindo, los corazones.

At midnight we walk home in the dark
and its moonlit snow to sleep

imagining glasses waiting to be filled
names ready to be emptied and adopted

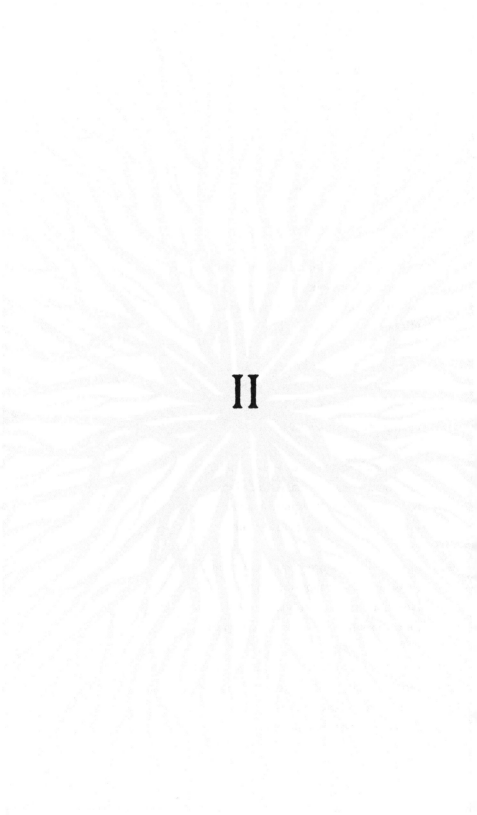

II

Debut

For the 27th Anniversary of D'Angelo's Brown Sugar

Praise the Montgomery Ward
stereo my mother spent
her first paycheck on, thrumming
with D'Angelo, brown sugar

a lull for prenatal-me, a bassline blessing
across every amniotic ripple. Colic
was my condition, cured by track two.
His falsetto reached, alright,

over terrible twos and threes, soulful
whine masking mine. If your voice
can't sound that good, why bother
talking at all? *Jonz in my bonz*

was an early search on dad's eMachine,
aged four, a Google Image education,
bodies in an 800x600 spread for me.
Finally those dreaming eyes of mine

open up, I begin to see and make sound
again, muted like cupped trumpets.
Now is a time of contrasts, five rests
for each sound. *Shit, Damn, Motherfucker,*

in that order, were my first swears, a habit-
forming drug, curses clattering out
of my mouth like snare snaps in sixth grade
classrooms, coarse language from smooth

faces. It was seven years ago that I
shifted from short story, lured from
Flannery to the song of individual
words, practicing assonance, cruising

across colonies of consonants.
Writing, song, art has been an act
of finding out how we sound again.
On that eighth day, when we get by,

when we are new again, words will
emerge sturdy from behind our canines.
We'll know how we carry music and vice
versa along the way, from grace and malady,

everything influential as decimals.
Line lengths like mixing boards,
I step up to the microphone believing
from here it only gets higher.

Willing Myself into Existence

I'm in an undergrad workshop,
aged sixteen, and afraid

of everyone else, the two-or-three
year gap between us a gulf

large enough, I think, to birth
judgment. My paranoid resentment,

my simultaneous respect and fear
of anything I see as more experienced.

So here I see enemies, red-eyed,
faces flush with disapproval, competition

for no prize. I am told again
and again that I'm too concerned

with other voices, and that my own
is absent. That I carve temples

out of someone else's unwilling
ribcage. That I am nowhere.

                    *

What I need them to understand
is that I'm not the only one in here.

How are we supposed to think?
Do you see the words in front of your inner eye?

Do you hear your own voice, familiar,
explaining yourself to yourself?

My "I" is new, it hasn't experienced much.
I don't know how I sound;

like in a home video, banded and green,
something with my face speaks,

and I have to ask a mom or cousin,
Is that how I really sound?

I think in everyone else's voice, alien
in my own mind, catching a few

who invited him looks from ones
who have been at the party longer.

Maybe I'm not just passing through.
But how do I become the house itself,

the venue and collection of crowd noise,
occasional voices breaking through then receding?

I don't know how to do this,
how anyone does.

*

But this is all unsaid. Instead, I
will manufacture an I

out of obligation for years,
and hope to find a real one later

in another body that has it figured out,
a body or mind that I may feel able

to call mine and christen *I.*

poem in which i avoid looking at my submittable account

call it *Schrödinger's Verdict* / the hope that / somehow i've earned it / the single verdant pop drowned / in clusters of gray and blue / but it's a microwave / with a roach in it / i can lie to myself as long / as i don't look / as long as / i bookmark novels with my poems / folded text-out between pages / like talent is transdermal / telling my lines to steal new tricks / when just out of sight but / they always come out / as dry as they went in / as long as i / stay away from me / the way i try / to give every animal i meet / a different voice but they all / end up stuck with my words / now this is the moment / for slouching / like ankles sunken in sodden sand / i imagine who this is for / in the first place / is there a journal of people like me / looking for this sort of work / if i were like me would i like me? / i think of how much / i dislike rhetorical questions / and draft a rejection letter in my head

Places I've Left Myself

This one is simple: *Y peeler*
                    smooth orange
                    pinky tip
                    an easy slip
I pick up a fingerprint
caught between blades
thin as shaved silverskin
and hold me in my hand

turn me over hide the ridges
and examine the under–
side strands that kept me
together. I toss myself

into the trash next to
cherry pits and apple stems
and wonder where else
I've been left

I'm in my aunt's basement
the child's head careening
into coffee table corner
turned an old blood umber

I'm in a lint trap in Hattiesburg
hair strands threaded through
her pillowcase and separated
by the dryer's tumble

I'm in the shower drain

of my childhood home
nosebleeds soaked between
screws like an archive of me

Now my blood is hitting the floor
and bouncing into grout
but I keep calm because
there's always pain

when you leave yourself.
This is no different. The pinky
will heal will look deflated and lose feeling
but at least I'll be somewhere

The Writer Upon Seeing His Reflection in the Screen While Watching The X Files

It's a series of nerds, bad hair
and band shirts, so naturally
he's wondered how he'd fit in.
In Connerville, Oklahoma
Giovanni Ribisi controls lightning.
In Miller's Grove, Massachusetts
the roaches fight back.
In Lexington, Kentucky the writer

didn't do the dishes so he sips
coffee from a measuring cup.
Surely he's played for a laugh
in the cold open, won't meet the stars.
He's surrounded by signifiers,

crumpled drafts and rejection letters,
rings of red wine at the bottoms of cups,
legs tangling at a computer desk.

He sees movement out the window
a crow tracing lines across the parking lot
a point of light that wasn't there before,
a trash can lid rattling alive,

nothing to worry about, so he keeps writing
humor to hide himself, includes a line
from an ex-girlfriend saying he looked
"reasonable." He self-deprecates
because it's sillier to be serious.

A sound from the alley like the crack
of hot ceramic on cold marble.
To check is to un-joke himself
for a moment, so he goes downstairs

and finds the episode he won't be a part of.
He's inciting incident, first blood, mutation
or the call for help as it goes black.

Then that theme song whistle pierces
like theremin, like ultraviolet
strong enough to whiten
teeth and singe brain cells.
Enough to make him believe
a fluke could find him vulnerable
and alter his story arc.

This is the lure of every episode,
the confidence the agents can escape,

reverse the old age makeup,
recover from alien pathogens

in forty-five minutes or less.
What keeps him suspended

like tractor beams are those like him
on the wayside, the day players

under-fives, like him
who don't return.

Missives to the Mirror Hanging in the Bar Bathroom

i'll just be a minute has turned into five
long enough to shout *oh*
                the hubris of Club Nouveau
        the mirror mocking my head

      shake
to the new beat of Lean On Me.
                i remind me that our toes
          are for balancing that we're brothers
           i'm ignored

he white knuckles the sink.

i tell him that we're hiding
          he agrees, yes, but i
                  need to get back out there

      he thinks we need another song first

    this track is too hard to handle
    is confusing us is a disagreement
    i say abomination but i say
    its the original, just unleashed

    there used to be two of me
        now one is disappearing
            into an embarrassment

of smoke scented clothes
pride swallowed with liquor
i'm in someone else's hands he is

hurting myself i am
asking us to stop poisoning me
he says we can drive himself
home soon and i say we can't

and this argument
is going nowhere

which makes we worse.

we have bruises
we don't recognize
we both can agree we need
somebody to lean on, wish

we could superimpose, overlay
us
on
us
like thin tracing paper
outlines altogether now
but we can work on that later

in the present
we don't know which
version will emerge from here
the club remix or Bill Withers'
but whoever it is will be

me   we   he   us   i

Ode to Hidden Tracks

For Vanilla Ice

To The Extreme's first track
gets all the air, it floats
to the top, breaches thick
surface enough to suck
from Mercury and Bowie.
This is the one he is proud of.
But I want to pipe oxygen
to the bottom feeders, drop
bubbles for the deprived
tracks two thumb scrolls down.

> A call to action: I implore you to take out your phone right
> now and listen to "Havin' A Roni" by Vanilla Ice. It's only
> about a minute, I'll check back in when you're done.

Welcome Back
Before streaming they were unnamed,
unlisted, only heard after everyone
had left, forgot the tape was still turning,
seconds of silence rewarded with—

well for Mr. Van Winkle
it's beatboxing.
I wanted you to hear this
because he didn't.

That silence is a pop filter,
clarifying and swelling plosives
like an inflating gum, casting out
the treble highs and thin listeners.
When he returns he speaks
to us in an indecipherable
vocal tap code, and for a moment

it feels like we are in on a joke,
arcing our head into another room
and catching someone's eyes,
maybe a quick upward nod.

The hidden track is direct address,
it is a child hearing their name
over the school announcements
and knowing that something
is just for them.

What Vanilla Ice has to offer
is to hear him distilled, no hook,
no DJ revolving, just man

and mic, exhibition of
what he can do on his own.

Scatting is what he was saving
for the dedicated. And now,
you're in on the joke too.

Special Guest Writer: My Notes App

I've moved into an apartment
near a hospital and my notes feel
the life-flights every night, they muse
about "how buildings break into us,"
these outside sources of emotion
like helicopter blades strong enough
to "vibrate nails out of walls," joists
like elbows digging into our ribs.
This is excavation, chipping away

to find a bone or stonework,
anything worth anything.
I can't just throw them away,
leave them to the cold press
of highlight and backspace.
The text writhes, pulses from stimuli
it only grows. I've made it a mission
to delete something only when I find
a use for it. It's becoming unwieldy.

So I will machete "lines like vines," chop
"thumbnail into touchscreen" to plumb
my used-to-be's and purge them.

The app's long lines and blue period
are from a breakup years ago;
I can track my brand of depression from image,
from the mope of "garbage pickup = sisyphean?"
and "always a fly in the room (unable to be happy?)"

They bounced back, became whimsical
in their comfort, performed shameless standup
about Stelara commercials and their colon mascot:
it's light work, but it's there.

The notes deserve to live somewhere
else, because these words, typed
in a voice no longer my own
have weight so I let the words sleep
with windows open, let them pick up
what they want or be carried by
whatever breeze needs them.
When I wake, hopefully a few lines
have wafted across the street or beyond,
have found somewhere better to be.

I Am Blackout at This Party and Complaining About The Chainsmokers

What I've heard is secondhand but I recall the high throb, guys aged thirty-and-counting singing I remember I am twenty-one and under all that we are razing each other's writing on couches arced like guts until my words swell until I excuse myself until I am lying on the florid shower curtain they dragged me out on I am mercifully spotless I am ruining this party and I am criticizing the playlist I am aware that a sixer of Christmas ale at eighteen will have mom tossing Kings Hawaiian across the room at me to sop the 7.5% churn of spice I am learning to stop drinking before my teeth feel fat I am also learning that thirteen lagers in three hours is my limit and passing it means passing out I am learning that they took my keys I am learning that a low-point has a soundtrack and I have notes for the musicians I am learning that I am already the old man whining about auto-tune as I sick-sweat silhouette into my shirt and everyone is rushing in after I tip over and take out the towel rack and I am only getting older but this is supposed to be from someone younger I am learning that they are unbothered as Charlee says she finds it more funny than sad and they wedge throw pillows under me and clean sheets dance static on my skin but I am learning that I cannot wedge a pencil into a brain wrinkle to excise these moments I am learning that what I resent is confidence and I am learning that they can move without failure guiding them I am learning that I hate how they've made their mistakes invisible but I am learning that I want this mistake to be invisible I am learning that I shouldn't be in charge yet I am aware that this can't happen again but how can I learn if the lesson is gone—

Keys clinked in the bowl,
this moment can drive, because
I am still learning

The Ghazal I Asked For

After Larry Levis

I will light novels on fire, hold them high, let syntax drip
onto my chest, crisp like hot wax on skin, old burnt words

I will collect texture, take scuffs from brick, pull hangnails
Blindfolded, I will read like braille the world's hurt words

I will lie naked on wet gazettes, osmose an aria from touch
hope that it works; that on my skin there will lurk words

What to do with these words; arrange them? Play Tetris
with image, hold an adverb, flip familiar, overheard words?

I will work from taste, find my way from zest and stale air
I will sit at the edge of the bed. You will kneel: her words

I will hold until the moment to make something worth something
I learn to love pain, hope I have deserved or earned words

I will pull the words from my skin. I'll bind and sign them
Alfonso Zapata. I give you all I have, and now they're your words

Palm Reading

I wish I was an NBA player because then I'd never
have to wonder what to do with my hands
in a picture but here I am palm sweat pooling
in the lithe curves of a keyboard beading on *I*
I shake people's hands and venture into their skulls
to see instinctive flinch tongue scraping the backs of teeth
as they wipe their hand on their leg *sorry about that*
I stand fidgety because I have a rotation:
fold arms until the sleeve and side darken
pocket them like something illicit until wallet softens
rest them on thighs until their shadow sticks
after moving rinse with cold water repeat
and other times the medication works to crag
my skin dehydrating until lifelines are ravines
and I wonder what rough future a palm reader
would tell for me do they see that when I write
the words appear smeared and bleed
on my hand heels and notebook lines blur
making me the medium credited on placards
as *Damp Canvas?* But I can stop this spiral
because what we make mimics us
like transmission towers' raised arms
like cars and their eyes and ears
like trimmed trees part for power lines.
Every awkward affliction a collage of reason,
my writing comes from all these limbs

All Our Lives: Track 1

[Play] Foo Fighters

Three-Stacks raps *She Lives*
In My Lap, but Grohl would like
to swap the subjects
for a tongue tip's sizzle, lisps
of sibilant driven love.

Why be sly: the song
is about cunnilingus.
Can you feel it now?
Palm-mute's throb, building up, pulled
back. Done. Let the drumsticks fall.

[Pause]

> *Here, I come to you,*
> *reader, as a listener.*
> *Nothing up my sleeve,*
> *I am separate from them,*
> *apart just as you and I.*

[Skip Track]

All Our Lives: Track 2

[Play] Linda Ronstadt with Aaron Neville

Is there a you, or
just a to-be-determined;
searched for, life handed
over to an abstract one,
a song as a substitute?

Here's your cue. Your chaste
reminder, *hey*, breaks through bridge
gifting a promise
of Aaron's wavering wind.
Live for you, only for you.

[Pause]

> *I examine as*
> *a seeker trying to find*
> *something I don't have,*
> *searching in art, using words*
> *of another to fill in–*

[Skip Track]

All Our Lives: Track 3

[Play] K-Ci & JoJo

Insecurity
is a natural state; do
we all need our loves
to be ordained by the grace
of strings and ethereal

choir cries, render
the beat obsolete? Compare
with other loves, need
to thank God, pray that you'll stay
together til the fadeout.

[Pause]

> *-the blanks, force my voice*
> *into someone else's mouth.*
> *I'll stop the music*
> *at last to assert myself.*
> *What love, if any, is here?*

[Stop]

The Writer Attempts to Paint

Layer -1: Evoke

The Artist hasn't painted since
hand turkeys in elementary
and washable pointillism
in middle school.

The Artist acts at a distance
and dislikes art talk; he pictures a brain
seeping blue fluid when painters explain
themselves, prefers the worker, discussion
of labor and technique, considers Bob Vila
the most interesting artist. The Artist
doesn't want to be The Artist, so he isn't.

The Artist shall be heretofore referred to as
The Writer.

The Writer isn't aiming high. He doesn't wish
he could paint green grapes like clouded eyes
or too-proud men standing at pointed cliffs of sublime
or hairs dripping from the napes of necks.

The Writer is a poet so he starts with phrases
something he thinks evokes, considers:

Johnny on the spot?

        Too easy, a man on a circle, anybody can do that

I expected more of you?

        Stop whining for once

Nice to meet you?

        ...

        Now there's something.
        Could be good or bad
        vague enough to flex
        to any interpretation
            art meeting audience
            collaboration
            the sides of The Writer merging

        ...

    third times the charm
    he supposes

so he heads out to meet someone

The Writer Attempts to Paint

Layer 0: Supply Run

The Writer can barely hold a pencil
like a human being. He starts with purchase,

> 12-Pack Deco Art Acrylic Paint: $14.99

carts past the brushes that remind him
of the tacky of the kitchen his family sponge-
painted four different colors before giving up.
The Writer sees enough to know
he knows very little about this process,
gets scared by the concept of Gesso.

> 2-Pack Simply 11"x14" Canvas: $8.99

He decides he hates this, he decides
to go abstract like Wall Magic so he treks
to the cleaning aisle

> 3-Pack Scotch-Brite Scrub Sponge: $3.49

and he wants his work to weigh
to reflect effort, to feel un-delicate
to raise itself like a welt from white

> Red Devil 6-in-1: $11.50

The Writer wants the words on the canvas
but this can't be poetry,
he imagines what this art has:
you can't scrape poetry, your words
are flattened no matter what you do,
so he finds something new

Surebonder Mini Glue Gun: $8.99

He checks out, drives home,
lays out old wrapping paper
across his office, spreads his tools.
Out of old carpentry habit
he takes his shirt off
ignores the mirror
and gets to work.

The Writer Attempts to Paint

Layer 1: Foundation

The Writer can't draw either
but he knows how to splash
a figure so he swipes
sponge through daubs
of green and black he lets
their bodies find themselves
sprout shoulders or
wings or wisped waists like
drifting like floating but

a foundation needs to stay still
he scours shaves paint into canvas
until its weaved skin wears down
and the bodies settle flat
as his words into scrapes
here is where they start
here is the distance between
here is a problem invented
for the solution

The Writer Attempts to Paint

Layer 2: Chewable

It is time to make good on
nice to meet you: he begins
to build an acrylic bifrost
across their gulf, it is time

to put that variety pack of paint
to work. He dots each figure's
side with bright glass eyes, splits
warm from cool, another
conflict that only exists
for the resolution.

He equips the 6-in-1. It fits
the hand better than a brush,
   he's pried caulk lines like taffy
   he's extracted wood nails like teeth
   he's scraped grout like icing
so he does what he knows:
presses its metal jaw into surface,
guides color toward each other
lets it pile in the middle

but paint doesn't dry quick enough
for what he wants, keeps falling,
a naturally occurring issue, unplanned,
so he rolls pencils up to the center,
cements them with paint as dams,
let the connection between these two
grow tall, gain a form thick enough
to chew.

The Writer Attempts to Paint

Layer 3: uh oh it isn't working

The Writer used to have two nice blobs on the canvas / they kind of
looked like people to him wafting silhouettes / now he has one blob
that looks like what it is / colors thrown together like a child / was
told to clean his room that morning / and mom is coming to check
/ but he forgot and he can hear her footfalls / so he shoves clothes /
and Sum 41 CDs under the bed / like that'll be enough / a canvas as
clumsy as multicolored tees / tangled and mounded hoping no one
will check / paint puddled up bordered by / bedsheet white and now
/ this is a period of doubt. He flips the painting over and hides his
shame for a week / he sees a Michaels ad for paint supplies / and they
make it look so easy / he feels worse / but he looks at the painting
again / flipped he sees the backside / the honest beige of fabric / it
reminds him that canvas / is woven is cloth is peppered / with its own
pigment / he likes the color so he flips / the painting again / spills his
coffee on a corner / The Writer calls this *texture* / and he is interested
again / he thinks he can finish this

The Writer Attempts to Paint

Layer 4: One Interpretation

A glue gun is essentially a syringe
The Writer uses to inject a word

make language intravenous
let it carry the weight he wants

so he pipes the letters, rises them
like scabs, like this art is self-inflicted

a wound to be healed.
He scribbles in golf pencil around

the letters like they oozed smoke
like scarring, like a mending suspended

and peels them up with a butter knife
because for him it all must be blunt

art must hit you with a hammer
and walk away must throw coffee

on your good jacket must be the question
and the answer at once must look good

in the process must stand up for itself
must be able to exist without him

and all these musts were mysteries
until that Meijer trip

he has not met someone new
he has met himself

in new lighting new colors cast
across crevices in his hands

and even back in the sick yellow
glow of his apartment he still sees

these colors after washing up
he listens to Sum 41 again

pulls shirts from closets
and pools them on the floor

hammers a nail into lumber
and pulls it back out

c-clamps the distance
between me and him.

Nice to meet you

This was not a meeting
this was a reunion.

III

The Warmer The Wind

Wind blows the blind pull-string
        into a guitar
        and strikes a chord
        I've never heard

Wind blows dried hornets
        from their window
        trap to land
        in my damp hands

Wind blows warmer this winter
        and we will say this
        every year until
        it parches our throats

Wind blows mold spores
        from fuzzed leaves
        in an attempt
        at biological warfare

Wind blows slivers through
        AC condensers
        to slow erode
        its whirring mimics

Wind blows in textures
        to fan a tarot deck
        and illustrates us
        in unflattering flutters

Wind blows and we try
       to echo it in our mouths
       but only amount
       to whispers

Wind blows and kicks up dust glinting
       in amber sunlight
       and animates
       our fading shadows

Wind blows or breathes
       four degrees hotter
       and makes its point
       to an empty room

INT. DIVE BAR — NIGHT

NAMUS STATISTICIAN
██████ individuals go missing every year. █,██
unidentified bodies are recovered each year.[1]

A man is dormant in the back booth haggard with wind split
lips leaning back like laughter like his breath has been pulled
taut from behind and there's no blood but there's nothing else
either and the investigator will avoid eye contact like he was a man
on the street with a cardboard sign because for all he knows he is.

CHIEF MEDICAL INVESTIGATOR
The number of unidentified bodies... across the ██████
██████ — it's like a mass fatality, except it's a quiet one.[2]

---

1 "The Extent of the Problem," NamUs, accessed May 9, 2024, https://namus.nij
.ojp.gov/about#the-extent-of-the-problem

2 Halber, Deborah. "What Happens to a Dead Body No One Can Name?,"
The Atlantic, last modified May 18, 2016, https://www.theatlantic.com/science
/archive/2016/05/john-doe-jane-doe/482961/

INT. ███████ FULFILLMENT CENTER — SUNSET

OSHA DIRECTOR

The six workers who died and others who were trapped or injured were all in a bathroom... it was designated as an emergency gathering area, it was not reinforced to hold up against an EF-3 tornado.[3]

Cloud lips purse for a spit take shower and squall whips oaks scalps steel from any shack so the box sealers and forklift drivers huddle at their conveyers put the tornado siren's waver aside need the deskspace for enough bubble and crisp paper to break your hairdryer's fall from the sky where they'll all be pulled into soon with expedited shipping.

 ECONOMIST

The time to do the drills is also time they are not moving the packages... But I don't think any company wants to harm its employees.[4]

---

3 Landis, Kelsey & Koziatek, Mike. "OSHA Releases Results of INvestigation into Edwardsville Amazon Warehouse Tornado Deaths," last modified April 27, 2022, https://www.bnd.com/news/local/article260767932.html

4 O'Brien, Matt. "OSHA Opens Investigation after Amazon Warehouse Collapses During Tornado, Killing 6," last modified December 13, 2021, https://www.pbs.org/newshour/economy/osha-opens-investigation-after-amazon-warehouse-collapses-during-tornado-killing-6

INT. MINE SHAFT — DOWN THERE
WHO CAN TELL

MEDICAL EXAMINER

Of the ▮ men killed, ▮ died as a result of ▮▮▮ 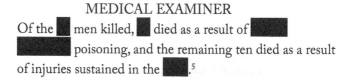 poisoning, and the remaining ten died as a result of injuries sustained in the ▮.[5]

When you pierce the earth you'll hit water eventually but what we need is deeper than that so pump the water out and because what we need will spitfire the air you'll need fans to breathe but because what we need is pricey cut the fans and take shorter shifts but because what we need takes metal on rock the air that isn't air anymore only needs one spark to-

THE FORMER COAL CEO ▮▮ ▮▮▮▮ 3 YEARS AFTER

Miners deserve the safest coal mine that truth and technology can give them.[6]

---

5 United States, Governor's Independent Investigation Panel, "Upper Big Branch, The April 5, 2010, explosion: a failure of basic coal mine safety practices". West Virginia, 2011.

6 @DonBlankenship. "Miners deserve the safest coal mine that truth and technology can give them. They aren't getting either today. We need to change that." Twitter, January 8, 2013, https://twitter.com/DonBlankenship/status/288856377059860480

The Produce Department Feeds the Hole in the Wall

we sink our thumbs   into cara caras, let them

    unclot themselves over

        empty apple crates

stroke fruiting fungus   caked on strawberry calyx

    crack knuckles of celery

        as we cart them to the compactor

            Department 99 is now open
            sounds over loudspeaker
            like a church bell

      Its mouth measures 2′x2′
      gnashes flicks its cardboard
      tongue across hands
      and we waste

    we rotate
        stock FIFO style
    we check
        raspberry ID for sell-by date
    we report
        the man pocketing a pear

we feed

        pears to 99 the next morning

  we lock

      our dumpsters

because we must love the mouth   keep it safe by speaking in code
give it what we can't have   wait for it to chew
sever its saliva strings   wipe its lips and bring it more

the mouth of the department
the only one fed for free

Directives to the Midwest

bring a little casserole to work
in the plastic container you got
the dumplings in yesterday

have your son hold the light
while you swap a serpentine belt
and teach him how to read a dipstick

wake up parched at three am and learn
that this was your worst mistake. watch,
from a hospital, the president mime a sip

attend a town hall meeting
field questions from warblers
flee the VFW from worker bees

never needing nails clipped eau de
Fast Orange any length of ladder you need
the Tyvek taken from the job site might save your life

scrub the water spots the dishwasher left
ignore the growing black
at the end of every faucet

ladies and gentlemen of the jury who
has the right to let bolts loosen who
has the right to darken your skies

vote. but if you can't vote
(child, felon) we will still find you
deserving of your neighbor's sentence

when your small town becomes
a search engine suggestion
what do you do

its RSI that weakens your wrists
its writs written to release regulation
in sick legalese, its all it takes

and takes until your joints are joists
too pricey to fix so you'll be left to dryrot
til the roofs cave
til train brakes give way

In the laundry room while landlords empty the quarters

i hear my money
        jingle
        as they discuss
            their migratory patterns
                sarahs on a two week cruise around europe

                    been there before but at this time of year
                    its truly special

                sent pics of the leaning tower of pisa

            and kathys been there too took the same photo

                        sunburnt skin pretending to hold it up
                        like they were wanted there
                        like they were necessary

                bev

        gushes about greece

    its buildings bulbous and white as

    these malfunctioning washers

    the two laugh at how little they know
    about the machines how much work
    they get from the maintenance guys

and thats nice and all
but i'm
wringing tees because the dryers dont work
as the two swish between rows of us
invading coin slots like clamped mouths
and emptying drawers
pretending not to notice my
should i get out of your way

im trying to make the eye contact
they refuse because they know

its our names on their tickets

its the guessed names on bev's letters
Alfonso Zapata   or current resident
its the names of those who tripped during
rent hikes and the always encroaching skimp

hoping we didnt notice   when the laundry sign
switched out   and came back a quarter steeper

and here's our leaning tower   of people
when we finish   our slouch when we
hunch too   topple over

i hope we hit them first

We deadhead

phlox every fall, gather stems
into a magenta ponytail to guillotine
with garden shear, pollen spewing
ochre over our stained hands
as old blooms drop. I ask my mother *why*

do we deadhead?
She says *this little cruelty*
is a necessity, because the infinite
isn't enough, because sun and rain
when spread among so many
can only reach so far. And we
could water more, we could
split them and give them other air
we could find space in the house
or neighbor's gardens for them
to shelter but still we find them

and we deadhead.
I used to well up at the callousness of it,
the death of old phlox and their unsteady burst
of anthocyanins. But worrying is a chore
so we speed up as heat rises until
no hand is steady. One of us slips
and new growth gets clipped too. But we
continue, with newfound blindness

to what we deadhead.
I imagine carelessness: children
as they scribble across streets

and cars' approach; the cheap
wires holding apartments
together, the tired hand closing
distance, each of us one of a hundred
little stemmed lights, waiting

to be deadheaded.

Yellowdog[7]

I am of a species that needs
break rooms, that is so thankful
for psychology-tested wall colors
and the familiar spiral of carpet.

I am of a species as low profile
as jackhammers, that carves
signatures 300 meters deep.
I am of a species with a history

of self-sabotage, of irreversibles,
unbreakable contracts. But

you never signed anything.

Feel like a ghost, glimpse
the end: walk through Yellowdog.

Run hands through paint chips,
kick across toys dropped
and never picked up,
remainder of life in empty space.

I want to turn everything back.
I want to rejuvenate a company town,

---

7 Adjective, derived from "Yellow-dog Contract" (a signed agreement between employer and employee that forbids a single breath of unionization), now derogatory. A suddenly abandoned town in Pennsylvania.

sever scrip at the joint, head off
the infection, re-home the abandoned

stuffed animals on dusted floors. I want
to rescue a dispute, un-taxidermy
the victims of bullets wet with poverty.
Reconstitute Blankenship's miners, suck

the umber saliva of earth back into the earth,
what can someone's signature do to stop you?

On Endings

With every new tenant
the apartments shrink
a tenth of an inch

with a landlord's best friend,
eggshell paint, streaking over
all signs of previous life,

wiping down curry stains,
covering unaddressed mold
and unlucky cockroaches.

I hope that the world lasts
long enough for the apartments
to be unlivable pinholes, to be remade

from nothing again and again, new
first coats of paint
to welcome more life.

I hope that the world lasts
long enough to run out
of phone numbers,

to roll over and delete us
and our childhood landlines
centuries after our last call.

Perishable Goods

Zip Code 43605: On January 6 2022 an explosion from a near-by oil refinery shook my grandparents' house.

Since construction started in '70, Davis Besse Nuclear Power Station has had ten incidents.

If we are what we eat
then we were trash, a habit
of dumping Coke-sodden
ice, from paper cups, down
the sink. I consider what we

were afforded: canned foods,
Country Time from scrubbed
molé glasses. Iodide pills were free
for our proximity to Davis Besse,
but we were never afraid

of the nuclear, its radii.
We feared our breath.
Where we lived
there was always a fire
on the horizon, our sky

a scribbled slick, courtesy
of the refinery four blocks down:
the price of affordable housing.
We saw steel, its shine inked
away, and thought of our air,
thick enough to chew.

We feared the exhale of Ford
and Daimler-Chrysler
where our fathers burned
years and smoked metal, fumes
to create cars that create fumes,

feeding flames for bologna-
and-white-bread wages.
They waved off hard coughs,
our young eyes strong enough
to detect uncertainty
in the lilt of an eyebrow.

My grandfather's
lungs depleted
my father earned
asthma we lived
days of algal bloom
of boil-water advisories
of great lakes dethroned
of drought and dry wells
of brush fires scraping numbers
off the backs of soccer jerseys
and we were lucky enough
to eventually leave, but
what's coming has everyone
in its doomed circumference.

I still hear the ice melting
in the sink, oblong shapes

losing grip and clinking
through U-bends, hear
where the water goes so
time is short. I consider
what we're forced to swallow.
I consider what we're forced
to make our children inhale
to pay for our next breath.

ACKNOWLEDGMENTS

The poems "The Ghazal I Asked For," "Leaving My Abuelos' Basement, Christmas Eve 2022," and "Leaving My Abuelos' Basement, Christmas Eve 2015" first appeared *in Sho Poetry Journal*, Vol. 3.

Poems "Debut," "Como me Duele," "Dendrochronology and the Art of Notetaking," "Moving A Hospital Bed Into The Living Room," "A Dedication," "Untitled," "Interpreting Light," "Leaving My Abuelos' Basement, Christmas Eve 1999," "Palm Reading," "The Warmer The Wind," "On Felling Sixteen Dying Trees," and "Perishable Goods" first appeared in the chapbook *Together Now* published by Belle Point Press.

ABOUT THE AUTHOR

ALFONSO ZAPATA is a poet living in Lexington, Kentucky. He received his MFA in poetry at The University of Kentucky, and has attended The University of Toledo and The University of Southern Mississippi, where he obtained his master's degree in poetry. He is the recipient of the Jim Lawless IV Poetry Prize, and the 2022 & 2023 University of Kentucky MFA Poetry Awards. His work has appeared in *Sho Poetry Journal*, and he is the author of the chapbook, *Together Now* (Belle Point Press, 2024). He can be found editing and re-editing supposedly finished poems in various coffee shops in the area.